MASSACHUSETTS

A PHOTOGRAPHIC PORTRAIT

First published in the United States of America by:

Twin Lights Publishers, Inc.
10 Hale Street
Rockport, Massachusetts 01966
Telephone: (978) 546-7398
http://www.twinlightspub.com

ISBN 1-885435-38-X

10 9 8 7 6 5 4 3 2 1

Front Cover: Deborah L. Diamond
Back Cover: Michael Hubley, Alan Murtagh,
Cynthia Cronig

Book design by:
SYP Design & Production, Inc.
http://www.sypdesign.com

Printed in China

Other titles in the Photographic Portrait series:

ACKNOWLEDGEMENT

This Massachusetts book is the result of an expansive group of talented individuals who spent untold hours laboring to put this outstanding collection into your hands. Twin Lights Publishers reviewed more than thirty-five hundred photo submissions from hundreds of professional and amateur photographers. Our panel of seasoned judges included Ann Fisk, the former director of the Rockport Art Association, Regina Grenier, a lead designer at Rockport Publishers and Paul Sylva, the publisher of Artists of Cape Ann, filtered through those photographs to painstakingly select and reach a consensus on the prize winners. First place winner William Mattern, second place winner Alan Murtagh and third place winner Margareta Thaute have honored us with their exceptional art. Sara Day of SYP Design and Production of Cambridge and Wenham, Massachusetts once again has designed a book that magically draws the reader from page to page. Author Stan Patey carefully studied each image and created insightful and interesting captions.

The cumulative effort of the publisher, all of the photographers, the judges and the designer are beyond measurement and we are indebted to each and every one of them for their part in this venture.

JUDGES

Regina Grenier

Regina Grenier is a graphic designer living in Gloucester, Massachusetts. She has a BFA in graphic design and currently works at Rockport Publishers directing visual art books in graphic design, interior design, and crafts. Regina does freelance design for several Massachusetts based companies. Her passions extend to painting and photography as well.

Ann Fisk

The daughter of two professional artists, Ann Fisk has spent her life in the art community. An artist in her own right, she directed the Rockport Art Association for eleven years. Currently she is involved in artistic, cultural and civic organizations in Rockport and in taking artists on painting trips to Europe.

Paul Sylva

Paul Sylva is a former social worker who left to start several businesses of his own. He has worked as a framer of pictures, run an art transportation service, run an art reproduction house, been a fish dealer, owned two small breweries, consulted to the Kirin Co. in Japan and now publishes books. He has had a dream, however, to sail the Caribbean Sea. He now lives on his sailboat in the Virgin Islands.

Massachusetts has drawn adventurers to her shores perhaps since the legendary Leif Erickson sailed westward from Greenland to our continent around 1000 AD. Today, more than thirty million visitors to Massachusetts retrace the explorations of our historic guests annually. They travel the same coastlines that were explored by French and Spanish fisherman who reveled in the bounty of our fisheries, and by Giovanni Caboto (John Cabot) who surveyed the coastline in 1497 and 1498 to establish England's original claims to North America. They travel in droves to a bay formed by a long arm of land that was named Cape Cod in 1602 by Bartholomew Gosnold. Here they enjoy the sandy beaches and quaint villages.

In 1621 the first Thanksgiving was observed by the Pilgrims in their settlement of New Plymouth. Present day gives us Plimouth Plantation, a living museum where time is frozen in 1627. John Winthrop and a contingent of Puritans escaping religious persecution in England arrived in Salem in 1630 to join groups gathering together there from Cape Ann and other North Shore settlements. Many now travel to Salem and Boston's north shore to visit the House of Seven Gables and to learn about the witch trials of 1692. Modern visitors progressing northward will discover historic Gloucester Harbor and seaside communities like Manchester and Rockport along the striking coastline between Boston and New Hampshire.

Massachusetts grew steadily throughout the balance of the 1600s and early 1700s. Her coastal populations and settlers migrated westward across Massachusetts in search of farmland and room to pursue their dreams. The Boston Massacre in March of 1770 marked the beginnings of the American Revolution and led to the battles of Lexington and Concord in April of 1775. Driving west from Boston the battlefields of the revolutionary war, historic museums and national historic landmarks reveal the founding of our nation.

Massachusetts: A Photographic Portrait conveys a delightfully innovative vision of the Bay State as seen through the eyes of dozens of talented professional and amateur photographers alike. Stroll through the pages of this colorful and lively portfolio and take in the images of seashore and mountains, historic buildings and shimmering skyscrapers. Marvel at the tenacious lighthouses perched upon the ocean's edge, her enduring barns and farmyards, as well as the contrasts of her stark winters and luxuriant green summers. See the history of the state and of our country preserved in buildings, monuments and landmarks. Leisurely turn the pages of this chronicle considering each image, and absorb the color and perspective. Sense the history and drink in the splendor of Massachusetts portrayed here for you and let it become yours.

FIRST PLACE

BROTHERS MOSSING

SCITUATE

WILLIAM MATTERN
NIKON, KODACHROME F-4

William Mattern is a retired teacher, a sail maker, photographer, and painter. He has been photographing for over 25 years and has won many ribbons with his photos. His photography features seascapes using a variety of specialized techniques including sandwich slides and most recently, four images on a single slide using a unique method which he developed himself. Bill has been involved with the local waterfront scene most of his life and his artwork is a reflection of his background.

Poor fishing has driven these fishermen to harvesting sea moss to supplement their incomes. Sea moss, also known as Irish Seaweed, is collected from the rocks with long handled rakes. It is sold for cosmetics, medicines, and as a thickening agent in ice cream.

SECOND PLACE

FISHING BOATS

GLOUCESTER

ALAN MURTAGH
NIKON, FUJI F-11

The aging *Vincie N.* and *Rose Marie* sit idle at the wharves in Gloucester.

Born and raised in Wellington, New Zealand, Alan considers himself fortunate to have spent time in some of the most scenic areas of the world. He moved to Massachusetts a few years ago and was immediately impressed by the lighting of New England. "Nowhere is the legendary New England quality of light more apparent that at dawn, my favorite time to photograph," says Alan. Now a resident of Gloucester, Alan is compiling a portfolio of images of the beautiful Cape Ann area.

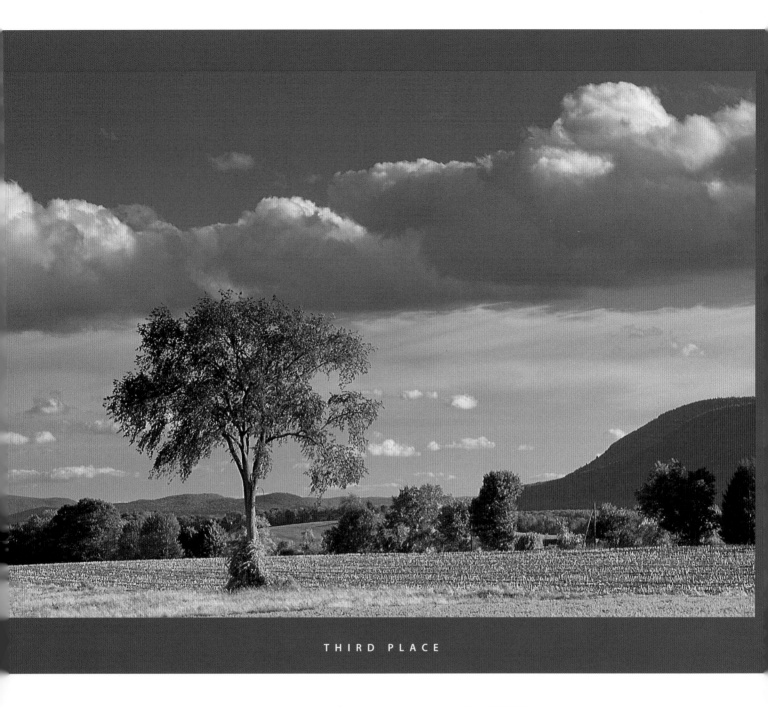

THIRD PLACE

MT. EVERETT

ERGERMONT

MARGARETA THAUTE
NIKON N90 S, FUJI PROVIA

A pastoral view of Southwestern Massachusetts and Connecticut beyond. The slope at the right is the lower elevation of the 2,608-foot Mt. Everett.

Margareta Thaute has had a lifelong interest in photography, but it was the beauty of the Berkshires, where she now lives, that inspired her to seriously pursue her interest. Western Massachusetts, with its rolling hills, rivers, lakes, birch trees and red barns, reminds her of her native Sweden, where she learned to appreciate the beauty of nature. Margareta's award-winning images have appeared in calendars, newspapers, *The Berkshires: A Photographic Portrait,* and other publications, and have been exhibited in numerous galleries in the Northeast. Her photographs are in many private and corporate collections.

CAPE COD STORM FENCE

CHATHAM

RICHARD D. GRAFTON
NIKON F-5, VELVIA F-22

Storm fences like this one near Chatham protect the fragile
sea grass and vegetation from being trampled. Once the vegetation is gone dunes are quickly eroded by the wind and sea.

SINGING BEACH

MANCHESTER

MICHAEL HUBLEY
NIKON F5, VELVIA F-22

Sunlight breaks through the clouds onto the rocks at Singing
Beach in Manchester marking the exit of bad weather.

QUARRY AT HALIBUT POINT

ROCKPORT

ALAN MURTAGH
NIKON, FUJI F-11

A winter view of the quarry at Halibut Point in Rockport. The former Babson Farm granite quarry is now a state park.

THACHER'S ISLAND

GLOUCESTER

ALAN MURTAGH
NIKON, FUJI F-11

Sunbeams penetrate the clouds beyond the North tower of Thacher's Island. The island, which is off the coast of Rockport, was named for Anthony Thacher and his wife. They were the sole survivors of a shipwreck on its shores in August of 1635. Twenty-one passengers and crew, including their children, perished.

NAHANT HOUSE

NAHANT

GORAN MATIJASEVIC

An ebbing tide at Nahant reveals the rocky shore line.

MAN AT THE WHEEL

GLOUCESTER

ALAN MURTAGH
NIKON, FUJI F-11

"They that go down to the sea in ships." The man at the wheel stands perpetual watch over Gloucester Harbor in memoriam for the more than 5,000 fisherman from Gloucester lost at sea since 1623.

FISHERMAN'S MEMORIAL

GLOUCESTER

DOUGLAS R. AMENDE
MINOLTA 700SI, FUJI VELVIA F-22

Gloucester's fishermen's statue originally entitled "Homeward
Bound," was commissioned in 1923. Local sculptor Leonard
Craske created the memorial, which was dedicated in August
of 1925.

SMITH ROCKS VIEW OF MINOT'S LIGHT

NORTH SCITUATE

WILLIAM MATTERN
NIKON, KODACHROME 64 F-5.6

The 114-foot-tall Minot's Ledge Light rises above the white-capped seas beyond Smith Rocks in North Scituate. This light is the second on the site and has been in service since 1860.

WHITE ELEPHANT ANTIQUE SHOP

ESSEX

DOUGLAS R. AMENDE
MINOLTA 700SI, FUJI VELVIA F-19

The White Elephant Shop in Essex opened in 1952
and houses the largest antique and consignment
shop north of Boston.

BURNHAM HOUSE ≫

ESSEX

ALAN MURTAGH
NIKON, FUJI F-11

The Mabel Burnham House on the marsh in Essex
speaks of simpler times. The house was converted
from a boat-building shop to a residence in the
1880's.

HOUSE ON THE MARSH

ESSEX

CHRISTOPHER WALTER
CANON EOS REBEL G, KODAK ROYAL GOLD 200

The Burnham House is often referred to as "Motif #2." The rustic building has stood untouched for years and was recently offered for sale.

EAST CHOP LIGHTHOUSE

MARTHA'S VINEYARD

DOUGLAS R. AMENDE
MINOLTA 700SI, FUJI VELVIA F-22

The East Chop Light was built in 1878 and had two predeces-
sors. The 40-foot-tall cast iron tower is located on Telegraph
Hill near Oak Bluffs on Martha's Vineyard.

ROCKPORT NORTH BASIN »

ROCKPORT

KEVIN AND SUSAN PSAROS
NIKON F100

Rockport's Motif #1 watches over the entrance to the North
Basin of Rockport Harbor. This fish shack is said to be the most
painted building in America.

BREWSTER BAY SUNSET

BREWSTER

SUSANNE M. CHAMPA
NIKON N8008S, FJUI VELVIA

The setting sun casts its glow on
Brewster Bay.

LANE'S COVE ≫

ESSEX

ALAN MURTAGH
NIKON, FUJI F-11

Gray storm clouds threaten lobster
boats safely moored behind the
seawall at Lane's Cove in Gloucester.

SAILBOATS ON THE MERRIMACK

NEWBURYPORT

KEVIN AND SUSAN PSAROS
NIKON F100

Sailboats moored on the Merrimack River in Newburyport.
The current is so powerful in this river that boaters plan their
comings and goings to correspond with the tides.

WEST FALMOUTH HARBOR >>

WEST FALMOUTH

DAVID F. GOUVEIA
NIKON, KODAK

Gaff-rigged sailboats wait patiently for the wind to push the
morning fog out of West Falmouth Harbor.

CAPE COD BAY FROM CAPE COD LIGHT

TRURO

JUDITH AUSTIN BROWN
KODAK

The Highland or Cape Cod Light was first lit in 1857, four years
prior to Abraham Lincoln's presidency. In 1996 the 404-ton
tower was relocated 450 feet inland due to erosion of the cliff
on which it was sited.

BOATS IN SUMMER

MANCHESTER

JOHN D. WILLIAMS
NIKON N80, FUJI REALA 100 F-11

The Emma Rose, a 36-foot Cal sloop, waits at the public floats
at Manchester Harbor for her charter. With all those dinghies
tied up, it must be a weekday.

BABSON FARM QUARRY >>>

ROCKPORT

MICHAEL HUBLEY
NIKON, VELVIA F-22

The mirrored surface of the quarry at Halibut Point State Park
perfectly reflects the sky. The Rockport Granite Company was
the last to work the quarry until they closed it down in 1929.

NANTUCKET SOUND

NANTUCKET

KIMBERLEY A. HOWLETT
CANON AE-Q, KODACHROME 100 250/F-8

An Invitation to Nantucket Sound. These storm fences channel
the way to the water while protecting the delicate dunes from
human steps.

EASTERN POINT LIGHT

GLOUCESTER

JOHN D. WILLIAMS
NIKON 6006, KODAK 100 F-8

This is the third light to be located at Eastern Point. It was constructed in 1890 and marks the beginning of the 2,250-foot Dog Bar Breakwater that protects Gloucester Harbor. Its beacon is visible some thirteen miles off shore.

GLASS PLATES

SANDWICH

MELLISA FRASER
CANNON EOS, KODAK GOLD F-5.6

Glass plates at the Thornton Burgess Museum depict the characters from the more than 170 children's books he wrote chronicling the adventures of Peter Rabbit and his animal friends.

REXHAME BEACH

MARSHFIELD

WILLIAM MATTERN
REBEL EOS, FUJI 100 AUTO

The prevailing winds appear to be gaining the advantage on
this storm fence in the dunes at Rexhame Beach.

MENEMSHA SUNSET ≪

MARTHA'S VINEYARD

PAMELA ECCLES
MINOLTA MAXUM 500SI, FUJI 400

A Menemsha lobster boat motors out into the sunset. Some
say that Menemsha means "still water."

ROWBOAT

ROCKPORT

JOHN D. WILLIAMS
NIKON 6006, KODAK 100 F-8

An experienced skiff saves a place at her master's mooring.

GOOD HARBOR BEACH

GLOUCESTER

MICHAEL HUBLEY
NIKON F5, VELVIA F-22

The rising sun and Salt Island bracket the creek at Good
Harbor Beach.

HOUSE AT GOOD HARBOR

GLOUCESTER

ALAN MURTAGH
NIKON, FUJI F-11

A grand home at the South end of Good Harbor Beach is silhouetted against the rising sun. Good Harbor Is an alteration of the original Native American title for the beach "Little Good Harbor" indicating that it wasn't a very good harbor at all.

COTTAGES AND FLOWERS

NANTUCKET

DOUGLAS R. AMENDE
MINOLTA 700SI, FUJI VELVIA F-22

A small roadway, reminiscent of another time, works its way between flowers and cottages in Siasconset, Nantucket.

FLOWERS AND GABLES «

SALEM

NANCY L. ROBISON
CANON, KODAK EXTRA AUTO

The raised flower gardens at the House of Seven Gables were designed by Joseph Chandler in 1909 to be an "oasis of beauty."

THE HOUSE OF SEVEN GABLES »

SALEM

BILL CRNKOVICH

Nathaniel Hawthorne was born in Salem on July 4th, 1804 and was inspired by The House of Seven Gables to write his novel about the mysterious mansion.

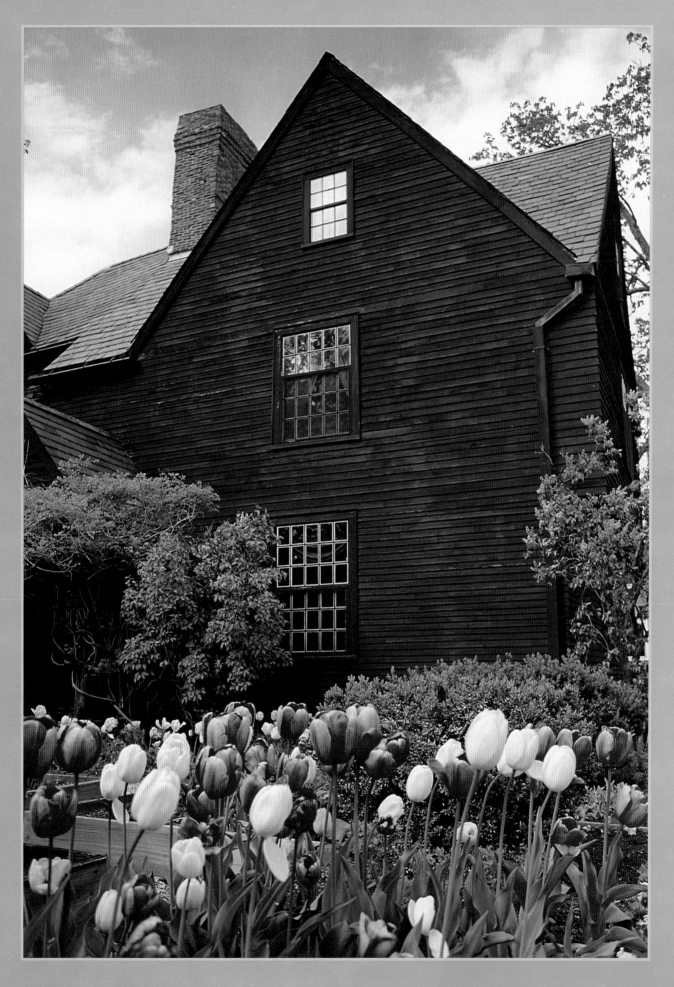

ROCKPORT SUNSET

ROCKPORT

MICHAEL HUBLEY
NIKON F5, VELVIA F-16

The coast of New Hampshire is visible along the horizon of
this sunset shot taken from the granite ledges near Halibut
Point.

LOOSESTRIFE INVASION »

PARKER RIVER, PLUM ISLAND

KEVIN AND SUSAN PSAROS
NIKON F100

This idyllic scene along the Parker River is illuminated by the
brilliant magenta flower of the purple loosestrife, an invasive
plant introduced from Europe in the 1800's. Unchecked, this
aggressive plant will take over all vegetation around it.

ROSE-COVERED COTTAGE

NANTUCKET

DEBORAH L. DIAMOND
F1 CANON, FUJI VELVIA F-8

Got Roses? Climbing roses spill over the fence bordering this Nantucket cottage.

FLOWERS ON NANTUCKET »

NANTUCKET

STANLEY CRONIG
CANON ELAN, FUJICHROME F-11

Vivid colors draw the viewer's eye to this weathered flower box on Nantucket Island

QUANT NEW ENGLAND «

NANTUCKET

DEBORAH L. DIAMOND
F1 CANON, FUJI VELVIA F-5.6

Roses climb the trellises along the cedar shingles of a Nantucket home.

MENEMSHA WHARF

MARTHA'S VINEYARD

DEBORAH L. DIAMOND
F1 CANON, FUJI VELVIA F-8

Freshly painted buoys top these lobster traps that are ready to go to work. Wire lobster traps have all but replaced the traditional oak traps.

SARGENT HOUSE MUSEUM ≪

GLOUCESTER

WILLIAM J. FERREIRA
PENTAX SPOTMATIC, KODACHROME 64

The Sargent House, now a museum, was built in 1782 for Judith Sargent Murray. She was one of America's first activists for women's rights. Her husband, Reverend John Murray, was the founder of Universalism in America.

SCHOONER "FREYA"

CAPE COD BAY

DONNA HACKLEY
NIKON F100, VELVIA

The sixty-three-foot schooner *Freya* on Cape Cod Bay hails out of Sesuit Harbor in Dennis and can be chartered for day sails and sunset cruises.

ROADSIDE GARDEN

NEWBURYPORT

MICHAEL HUBLEY
NIKON N90S, VELVIA F-16

A lovely garden upstages the gray sky background.

CHATHAM FIRE HYDRANT

CHATHAM

RICHARD D. GRAFTON
NIKON F-5, VELVIA F-22

Yellow wildflowers brighten the scene dominated by the richly colored hydrant.

HISTORIC MUNROE TAVERN

LEXINGTON

JAMES BLANK
PENTAX 67, EKTACHROME 64 F-16

During the Red Coat retreat from Concord, the Munroe Tavern served as temporary headquarters for Brigadier General Earl Percy and some one thousand British reinforcements. Although George Washington never slept here, he did dine here in 1789 when visiting the Lexington Battlefield.

NORTH BRIDGE ≪

CONCORD

KEVIN & SUSAN PSAROS
NIKON F100

The "Old North Bridge" stands at the spot where the colonial minuteman held off the British Regulars and turned them on their retreat to Boston.

REVOLUTIONARY RE-ENACTORS

SUDBURY

CYNTHIA CRONIG
MINOLTA, FUJICHROME F-8

Imagine the thundering blast of these authentic muzzle loaders. Battle Reenactments are frequent and colorful in Historic Massachusetts.

OLD IRONSIDES

BOSTON

ARLENE F. TALIADOROS
NIKON N90S, FUJI X-TRA

The U.S.S. Constitution is the oldest commissioned warship in the world. Launched in 1897, she was nicknamed "Old Ironsides" when, in battle, cannon balls bounced off her sturdy oak hull. She is one of the six original frigates of the U.S. Navy.

CAPT. JOHN PARKER ≪

LEXINGTON

JUDITH E. SINGER
PENTAZ 120 SW, KODAK 400

The statue of Captain John Parker was placed on the Green at Lexington in 1900 and is often referred to as the Lexington Minuteman Statue. Parker lead the colonial militia against the British regulars at Lexington on April 19, 1775.

CONCORD MINUTEMAN ≫

CONCORD

HELEN EDDY

The minuteman statue at the North Bridge in Concord depicts a farmer with his musket in hand. Completed in 1874, the Concord statue portrays a true minuteman with a plow at his feet ready to take up arms to defend his home at a minute's notice.

MASSACHUSETTS: A PHOTOGRAPHIC PORTRAIT 51

PAUL REVERE

BOSTON

NANCY L. ROBISON
MINOLTA MAXUM, KODAK EXTRA AUTO

The statue of Paul Revere is located near the Old North Church from which he was signaled with two lanterns to indicate the British expeditionary force was coming by sea. Revere rode toward Lexington by way of Charlestown neck to warn Sam Adams and John Hancock, as well as the country-side, of the British Regular's march on Lexington and Concord.

ROBERT GOULD SHAW MEMORIAL

BOSTON

ROBERT V. BEHR
MINOLTA SRT 101, FUJI F-11

This monument commemorates the 54th Regiment of Massachusetts Volunteer Infantry. Robert Gould Shaw, a white offi-cer from a prominent Boston family, vol-unteered to lead this first black regiment recruited from the North during the Civil War. For eighteen months the men refused to accept lower pay than their white counterparts. This regiment led an assault on Fort Wagner, South Carolina where they suffered heavy casualties but distinguished themselves for bravery.

OLD AND NEW ≫

BOSTON

GORAN MATJASEVIC

Trinity Church, consecrated in 1877, is reflected in the mirrored finish of the John Hancock Tower in Copley Square.

WEEKS BRIDGE

CAMBRIDGE

HELEN EDDY

Men's eights pass under the Weeks Bridge as they pull their way down the Charles River.

PARK STREET CHURCH »

BOSTON

LESLIE DAVIS
CANON ELAN 7, KODAK 100

Park Street church, located on the corner of Park and Tremont Streets, was constructed in 1809. It was once referred to as "Brimstone Corner" as gun powder for the War of 1812 was stored in a crypt in the basement of the church.

ZAKIM BRIDGE

BOSTON

JOHN ALDEN HALL

The Leonard P. Zakim Bridge is named for the former director of the Anti-Defamation League of New England. Zakim spent his life building bridges between people. The towers that top the bridge represent the Bunker Hill Monument.

SAILING DAY >>

EAST BOSTON

KEVIN AND SUSAN PSAROS
NIKON F100

Sailors furl the sails of their 23-foot Sonar Sloops at the East Boston Piers Park. The Park is a community sailing center created by Massport in 1995.

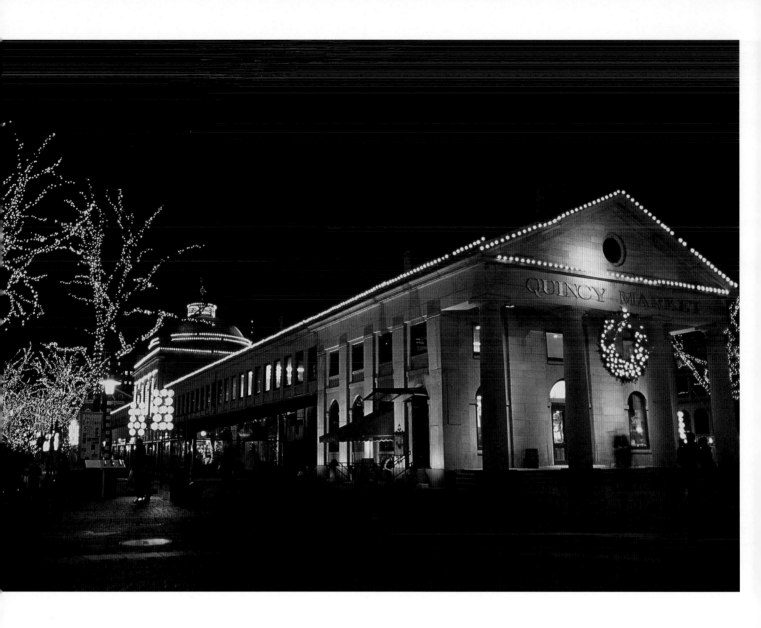

QUINCY MARKET

BOSTON

MICHAEL J. MCCORMACK
RICOH-KR5, KODAK ELITECHROME F-3.5

Built in the 1800's to serve as a wholesale food distribution center, Quincy Market is Boston's most visited tourist destination. The granite building was remodeled in the mid-1960's to accommodate food stalls serving everything from clam chowder and lobster to pizza and calzone.

CHARLES RIVER BASIN

BOSTON

MICHAEL J. MCCORMACK
RICOH-KR5, KODAK ELITECHROME F-5.6

A fleet of Mercury Sloops sail out of the Community Boating House near the Hatch Shell on the Boston side of the Charles River Basin.

BEACON HILL

BOSTON

MICHAEL J. MCCORMACK
CANON AE1, KODAK ELITECHROME F-22

Louisburg Square is perhaps the most prominent address on
Beacon Hill. Bow fronted Greek Revival row houses face each
other across a fenced in park that only residents may use.

COBBLE STONES

BOSTON

DOUGLAS R. AMENDE
MINOLTA 700SI, FUJI VELVIA F-22

Cobblestone streets, gas lights and red brick facades are
elements that distinguish Beacon Hill.

COMMONWEALTH AVENUE »

BOSTON

DAVID F. GOUVEIA
NIKON, KODAK

Wrought iron fences, rich green grass, bright flowers and
magnolia blossoms create a common springtime scene along
Commonwealth Avenue.

BOSTON COMMON BRIDGE

BOSTON

RICHARD ADAMS
NIKON N90S, FUJI VELVIA F-16

View of the pedestrian bridge crossing the lagoon at the
Boston Public Gardens. This bridge is said to be the world's
smallest suspension bridge.

HOLOCAUST MEMORIAL >>

BOSTON

WILLIAM MATTERN
CANNON REBEL, AQTA 100

Over 3000 organizations worked toward the 1995 dedication
of this memorial. One million serial numbers, representing the
Holocaust victims, are etched into each of the six glass towers.
These towers represent six chimneys of the Nazi death camps.

SWAN BOATS

BOSTON

HELEN EDDY

The Swan boats have carried visitors to the Public Gardens around the lagoon for more the 120 years. Powered by their pedaling captains, the catamarans cruise the lagoon from April to September.

MAKE WAY FOR DUCKLINGS »

BOSTON

HELEN EDDY

Robert McCloskey's ducklings Jack, Kack, Lack, Mack, Nack, Ouack, Pack, and Quack made famous in his book *Make Way for Ducklings*, are immortalized in bronze.

BOSTON HARBOR SKYLINE

BOSTON

HELEN EDDY

A twelve-meter yacht and a clipper ship are ornaments along
Boston's Rowes Wharf and the skyline along the harbor.

BEYOND THE CHARLES

BOSTON

MICHAEL J. MCCORMACK
RICOH-KR5, KODAK KODACHROME 64 F-16

The John Hancock and Prudential Towers rise above the Charles River Basin Shoreline as viewed from Memorial Drive In Cambridge.

HARVARD SQUARE ≪

CAMBRIDGE

LESLIE DAVIS
CANON ELAN 7, KODAK

Out of Town News at the kiosk at Harvard Square sells newspapers and magazines from around the world.

GLOUCESTER HARBOR

GLOUCESTER

MICHAEL J. MCCORMACK
CANON AE1, KODAK ELITECHROME F-22

Pleasure boats are moored in their slips in Gloucester's Inner Harbor. The East Gloucester waterfront is visible in the background.

PLIMOTH PLANTATION   >>

PLYMOUTH

JAMES BLANK
PENTAX 67, EKTACHROME 64 F-16

Visitors to Plimoth Plantation travel back in time to 1627 "New Plimoth." Re-enactors in period clothing assume the personalities of the original inhabitants of the colony.

TURNER HILL

IPSWICH

MICHAEL HUBLEY
NIKON N90S, VELVIA F-22

A keystone bridge is the focus of this winter scene taken on the Turner Hill Estate in Ipswich. Turner Hill was the Estate of Charles G. and Anne Proctor Rice. The mansion at Turner Hill was completed in 1903.

IPSWICH BROOK

IPSWICH

MICHAEL HUBLEY
NIKON N90S, VELVIA F-16

Bright fall colors reflect in a pond and brook at Turner Hill.
This former estate originally encompassed some 700 acres.
Presently the property is to be developed as a resort to
include an 18-hole golf course. The network of trails open
to the public is expected to remain intact and accessible.

WALDEN POND >>>

WALDEN POND

KEVIN AND SUSAN PSAROS
NIKON F100

"I think that each town should have a park...a common pos-
session forever, for instruction and recreation," Henry David
Thoreau wrote in an 1859 journal entry. In 1845 Thoreau built
a cabin near Walden Pond where he lived, studied and wrote.
His classic book *Walden* describes his experiences on the
pond.

OLD MILL

NANTUCKET

DOUGLAS R. AMENDE
MINOLTA 700SI, FUJI VELVIA F-19

The Old Mill was built in 1746 by Nathan Wilbur and is
believed to be the oldest working windmill in the nation. The
bright yellow flowers in the foreground are scotch broom.

JENNY GRIST MILL »

PLYMOUTH

DOUGLAS R. AMENDE
MINOLTA 700SI, FUJI VELVIA F-22

Pilgrim John Jenny built the original mill on this site in 1636.
The mill is operated by diverting water to the water wheel
which, through a system of cogs, revolves the grindstone.

CHATHAM LIGHTHOUSE AT SUNSET

CHATHAM

RICHARD D. GRAFTON
NIKON F-5, VELVIA F-22

The original light at Chatham was a set of two forty-foot-tall lights to distinguish them from the single Highland Light. A series of twin towers were built at the station, including replacements for two towers that slid off the eroding cliff. In 1923 one of the twins was moved to Nauset.

WHALEBOAT »

EDGARTOWN

DEBORAH L. DIAMOND
F1 CANON, FUJI VELVIA F-8

A classic whaleboat is displayed at the Old Sculpin Gallery in Edgartown. These double-ended boats were fast, light and maneuverable. While the crew pulled in close to their quarry the harpooner would stand in the stern at the ready.

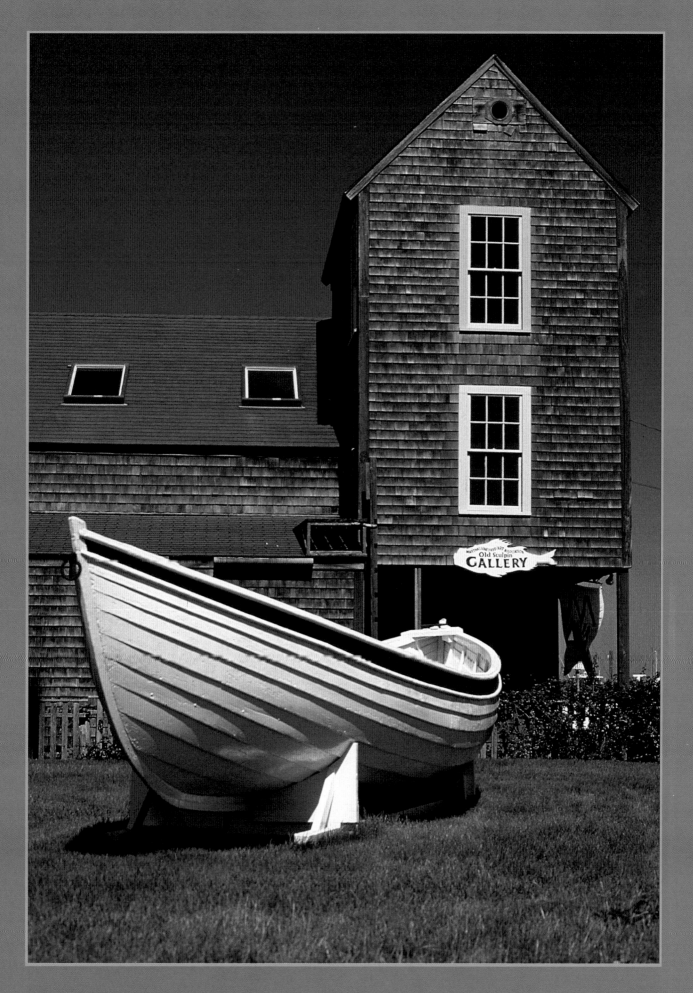

CAPE COD DUNES

SANDWICH

MICHAEL HUBLEY
NIKON N90S, VELVIA F-8

The wind has carved out paths through the ever moving
dunes at Sandy Neck Beach in Sandwich. On a clear day the
Pilgrim Monument in Provincetown can be seen across Cape
Cod Bay from this beach.

RACE POINT LIGHTHOUSE

PROVINCETOWN

DEBORAH L. DIAMOND
F1 CANON, FUJI VELVIA F-8

The Cape Race Light Station was established in 1816. The present 45-foot iron plate and brick tower was built in 1876. The New England Lighthouse Foundation invites the public to stay as guests of the lighthouse keeper at this station.

CRANBERRY BOG

CARVER

STANLEY CRONIG
CANON ELAN, FUJICHROME F-22

Cranberries grow in the bogs during the summer months. The berries contain air so the bogs are flooded to float the berries to the surface for the harvest.

CRANBERRY FARMER ≪

CARVER

MARIA GREEN
CANON REBEL

A cranberry farmer samples his crop. Cranberry cultivation began in Massachusetts around 1810 and is now the third largest agricultural commodity in the state.

NAUSET LIGHTHOUSE ≫

EASTHAM

JAMES BLANK
LINHOF, EKTACHROME 64 F-32

The Nauset Light is the former twin that was moved from Chatham in 1923. In 1996 the Nauset Light Preservation Society accomplished their goal of relocating the tower inland to save it from erosion.

Nantucket dinghies aground at low tide. The lines attached to their sterns are used to pull the boats ashore at high tide.

NEW BEDFORD LOBSTER BOAT

NEW BEDFORD

NANCY L. ROBISON
MINOLTA, KODAK EXTRA AUTO

Inshore lobstermen clean their boat. The gill nets in the foreground are made from fine monofilament nylon and are designed to catch fish by their gills.

CHATHAM BEACH

CHATHAM

RICHARD D. GRAFTON
NIKON F-5, VELVIA F-22

Wind and sea pile sand up along storm fences marking the
edge of sand dunes at Chatham Beach.

CAMPMEETING COTTAGES

OAK BLUFFS

DOUGLAS R. AMENDE
MINOLTA 700SI, FUJI VELVIA F-11

The Martha's Vineyard Campmeeting Association dates to 1835. The first members stayed in large dormitory type tents. Later on families would lease lots of land to pitch their own tents. In the 1860's and 70's the tents were replaced with cottages. There were some 500 cottages at the highpoint, now there are about 300.

WOODEN VALENTINE

OAK BLUFFS

DOUGLAS R. AMENDE
MINOLTA 700SI, FUJI VELVIA F-22

The Wooden Valentine House is among the many gingerbread homes that populate the Wesleyan Grove of the Martha's Vineyard Campmeeting Association. Note the Masonic, Shriner and Eastern Star symbols in the window.

OAK BLUFFS HOUSES

MARTHA'S VINEYARD

JAMES BLANK
PENTAX 67, EKTACHROME 64 F-11

Picturesque homes line the way at Oak Bluffs on
Martha's Vineyard.

SUMMERTIME PORCH

MARTHA'S VINEYARD

MARGARETA THAUTE
NIKON N90S, FUJI PROVIA

It's not difficult to picture yourself relaxing away a summer's evening on this colorful Martha's Vineyard porch.

VINEYARD COAST

MARTHA'S VINEYARD

JAMES BLANK
PENTAX 67, EKTACHROME 64 F-22

Nestled among wildflowers, a quaint cottage overlooks a spectacular stretch of the Martha's Vineyard coastline.

GAY HEAD »

MARTHA'S VINEYARD

JAMES BLANK
PENTAX 67, EKTACHROME 64 F-11

Gay Head or Aquinnah, as the native Wampanoag people call the area, is set apart by its colorful clay cliffs.

TRURO DUNES ≪

TRURO

JEFFREY J. HITCHCOCK
PENTAX K 1000, FUJI 100 F 8

The painted sky and wind swept dunes contend with each other to dominate the beauty of this shot taken off of Route 6-A in Truro.

PLEASANT BAY DORY

CHATHAM

JEFFREY J. HITCHCOCK
PENTAX K-1000, FUJI 100 F-4

A solitary dory rests in its own reflection at a Pleasant Bay lowtide.

OLD STURBRIDGE GARDNER

STURBRIDGE

THOMAS ROTKIEWICZ
CANNON ELAN II, COLOR NEGATIVE F-11

A gardener at the Old Sturbridge Village tends to his flowers.
The village is a non-profit organization depicting the life of
early New England between1790 and1840.

HARVEST »

WESTERN MASSACHUSETTS

JAMES BLANK
PENTAX 67, EKTACHROME 64 F-22.

A Western Massachusetts harvest.

QUABBIN WATERSHED

WARE

DARLENE B. BORDWELL
MINOLTA MAXIMUM, FUJI VELVIA

An old stone wall runs off into the lush woods that surround
the Quabbin Reservoir. In the 18th and 19th century, farmers
would clear the stones from their fields to build the walls that
marked their borders.

RTE. 112 BARN >>

BUCKLAND

DARLENE B. BORDWELL
MINOLTA MAXIMUM, FUJI VELVIA F-22

A failing Victorian barn survives to see another spring in
Western Massachusetts.

EDDY LAW OFFICE

SPRINGFIELD

BILL CRNKOVICH

The Big E or Eastern States Exposition includes a recreation of a 19th century village. This office was originally constructed circa 1810 in Middleboro and was moved to West Springfield. This Federal style building incorporates an arched copper roof and may be the only surviving example.

MT. HOLYOKE COLLEGE

SOUTH HADLEY

HELEN EDDY

Abbey Chapel at Mt. Holyoke College was built in 1897. The chapel was known as the Mary Lyon Chapel until 1937 at which time it was enlarged and renamed.

FIRST PARISH   >>

NORTHBORO

JANE PEDERSEN
NANNON ELAN II, FUJI SENSIA

The First Parish Unitarian Universalist Church of Northboro stands on the site of the original First Parish which was completely destroyed by a tragic fire in December 1945. The Parish decided to restore the church as it was originally built in 1808, but on a somewhat reduced scale. A surplus army chapel was purchased from the government in 1947 and moved from Bradlee Field, Connecticut to the church property in Northborough where it was rebuilt in accordance with the architect's plan for the Parish House. This building was dedicated on the twenty-seventh of June 1948.

SUNSET AT BEAVER BROOK

WESTFORD

DONNA HACKLEY
NIKON F-100, VELVIA

The sky is perfectly reflected in the still surface of Beaver Brook.

STURBRIDGE COVERED BRIDGE »

STURBRIDGE

CYNTHIA CRONIG
MINOLTA, FUJICHROME F-8

First snow at Old Sturbridge Village enriches this winter scene of the covered bridge on the Quinebaug River. Bridges were covered to protect the heavy beams and decking of the bridge. It was relatively inexpensive to replace the roofing and walls of the bridge. They actually shoveled snow onto the bridge to allow horse drawn sleighs across the bridge.

TICONDEROGA CANNON

NORTHBORO

GRENVILLE ROGERS

In 1976 a group of volunteers reenacted the transport of some fifty-nine cannon from Fort Ticonderoga in upstate New York to Cambridge by General Henry Knox. In 1776 the site of those canons high atop Dorchester Heights was sufficient to encourage the British to depart Boston Harbor.

WILD TURKEY
STURBRIDGE
GRENVILLE ROGERS

Benjamin Franklin nominated the turkey as the national bird, but of course, it lost to the eagle. The popularity of the bird as game decimated its numbers to about 30,000 birds in 1900. There are now approximately 5 million wild turkeys in the U.S.

STURBRIDGE COOPER
STURBRIDGE
GRENVILLE ROGERS

A re-enactor in the cooperage at Old Sturbridge Village demonstrates the trade of barrel building as it was done in the early 1800's.

NAUMKEAG'S BARN

STOCKBRIDGE

CAROLYN PEARCE
SEARS SLR, KODAK

A shot of the classic barn at the Naumkeag estate. It was built in 1885 as the summer home of Joseph Hodges Choate. The property is famous for its beautiful gardens.

BUTTERFLY >>

WESTFORD

DONNA HACKLEY
NIKON F-100, VELVIA

A butterfly rests on a flower inside the atrium at The Butterfly Place. You can walk through the 3,100 square foot atrium and view as many as 50 different species native to New England.

NORTHBORO BRIDGE

NORTHBORO

GRENVILLE ROGERS

The symmetry of this masonry bridge draws
your eyes to its beauty.

SANTARELLA MUSEUM ≪

TYRINGHAM

MARGARETA THAUTE
NIKON N90S, FJUI PROVIA

Santarella was designed and built by Henry
Hudson Kitson, the sculptor of the Lexington
Minuteman Statue on Lexington Green. This
was Kitson's studio and is now a museum
showcasing his growth as an artist.

BASIN BISH ≫

BERKSHIRES

MARGARETA THAUTE
NIKON N90S, FUJI VELVIA

These falls are located in the Bash Bish Falls
State Park in Mt. Washington, Massachusetts.
These dramatic falls have a drop of more than
eighty feet.

FRESH SNOW

ERGERMONT

MARGARETA THAUTE
NIKON N90S, FUJI PROVIA

Freshly fallen snow frosts a split-rail fence. The town of
Egremont is located in the Southwest corner of the state
and was originally settled by Dutch farmers.

YESTERDAY'S CABIN

NEW MARLBOROUGH

MARGARETA THAUTE
NIKON N90S, FUJI VELVIA

Grass and weeds are steadily overtaking this abandoned cabin in New Marlborough. This Southwestern Massachusetts town was opened for settlement in 1735. The first settler was Benjamin Wheeler who drew lot number twenty-five among the seventy-two land grant lottery winners.

GLACIER POTHOLES

SHELBURNE FALLS

ROSLIE FROST
CANON EOS A2E, EKTACHROME 100 F-22

Fascinating rock formation and potholes sculpted by retreat-
ing glaciers lie exposed below Salmon Falls on the Deerfield
River. The waters are periodically diverted to allow viewing of
the geology from an overlook.

PULP HOOK

WILBRAHAM

DOUGLAS R. AMENDE
MINOLTA 700SI, FUJI VELVIA F-22

A pulp hook left behind in a Wilbraham fence post. Pulp hooks are used by loggers for handling smaller logs by hooking into the end of the log with this tool.

AUTUMN SCENE

OLD DEERFIELD

JAMES BLANK
PENTAX 67, EKTACHROME 64 F-16

Soak up the vibrant autumn colors in this shot of
the Dwight-Barnard House, a slate roofed example
of Georgian architecture.

RICHMOND BLISS

RICHMOND

MARGARETA THAUTE
NIKON N90S, FUJI VELVIA

Rich greens and blues enhance this photo of a
pond and field. Richmond was settled in 1760 and
named for Charles Lennox, the Duke of Richmond.

CONNECTICUT RIVER »

GREENFIELD

JAMES BLANK
PENTAX 67, EKTACHROME 64 F-11

The Connecticut River winds through the hills
of Western Massachusetts near Greenfield.

ROLLING COUNTRYSIDE

NEW ASHFORD

ROSLIE FROST
CANON EOS A2E, EKTACHROME 100 F-16

Rolling countryside along route 7 in the Berkshires.

MT. PROSPECT *(top)*

ADAMS

ROBERT V. BEHR
MINOLTA SRT 101, FUJ F-11

Mt. Prospect (2,690 feet) is viewed from the west of Mt. Greylock. The Taconic Range can be seen in the background. The Appalachian Trail runs over Mt. Greylock and Mt. Prospect.

RIPPLE SPREADING *(bottom)*

GRANBY

FRANK E. EATON
CANON T90, FUJI VELVIA

Early morning mist hangs over the pond at Dufresne Park in Granby. The park is a favorite for cross-country races, horse shows and family relaxation.

SHEFFIELD CEMETERY

SHEFFIELD

MARGARETA THAUTE
NIKON N90S, FUJI PROVIA

Aging grave markers in a Sheffield cemetery chronicle the
town's citizen's histories. Sheffield is a small Western
Massachusetts town with a population of slightly less than
three thousand that was settled in 1726.

APPLE BLOSSOMS *(top)*

GREAT BARRINGTON

MARGARETA THAUTE
NIKON N90S, FUJI PROVIA

A blossoming apple tree frames this Great Barrington Barn.

DWIGHT-BARNARD HOUSE *(bottom)*

DEERFIELD

DOUGLAS R. AMENDE
MINOLTA 700SI, FUJI VELVIA F-19

The Dwight-Barnard House was built in 1754 and is a classic example of Georgian Architecture. This style was in fashion starting in 1711 during the reign of King George I until the American Revolution and the reign of King George III.

CHURCH OF CHRIST

BERKSHIRES

MARGARETA THAUTE
NIKON N90S, FUJI VELVIA

The Church of Christ was organized in 1874. The tiny town of Mt. Washington was settled in 1692 and has a population of around 135 citizens.

ALFORD CENTER SCHOOL *(below)*

ALFORD

MARGARETA THAUTE
NIKON N90S, FUJI VELVIA

The Alford Center School now serves as the Town Offices. The town was named for Col. John Alford of Charlestown.

PRESIDENT'S HOUSE »

WILLIAMSTOWN

ROBERT V. BEHR
MINOLTA SRT 101, FUJI F-8

This Federal style home was built in 1801 and has housed Williams College presidents, including Mark Hopkins, since 1858.

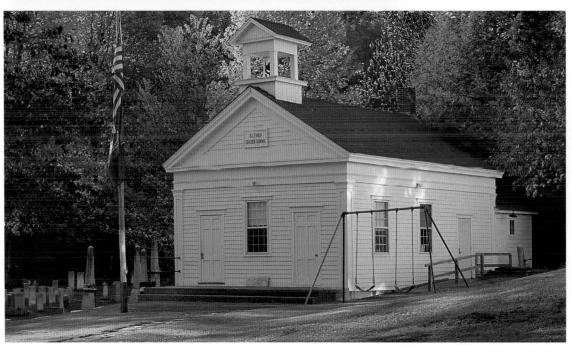

GREEN RIVER

WILLIAMSTOWN

ROBERT V. BEHR
MINOLTA SRT 101, FUJI F-8

The Green river in Williamstown frames the distant "Hopper," a funnel-shaped valley in the Mt. Greylock massif in the northern Berkshires.

TYRINGHAM BARN

TYRINGHAM

MARGARETA THAUTE
NIKON N90S, FUJI VELVIA

Why are so many barns red? Most of this dates back to when farmers mixed their own paint from linseed oil, lime and even milk they would add ferrous oxide (rust) which was inexpensive and protected against rot and produced a nice red color.

SHEFFIELD BARN >>

SHEFFIELD

MARGARETA THAUTE
NIKON N90S, FUJI VELVIA

Cows graze in the foreground while the barns and silo in the background are framed by a beautiful weeping willow.

GRIFFIN HALL

WILLIAMSTOWN

ROBERT V. BEHR
MINOLTA SRT 101, FUJI F-16

Griffin Hall at Williams College was built in 1828 for a cost of $6,000. Constructed in a Federal Style of architecture, the building serves as classrooms.

WEST COLLEGE

WILLIAMSTOWN

ROBERT V. BEHR
MINOLTA SRT 101, FUJI F-11

This present day dormitory was the original college building at Williams. It was built in 1793 and houses forty-four students.

FARM RELIC

EGREMONT

MARGARETA THAUTE
NIKON N90S, FUJI PROVIA

A rusting dump rake, circa 1900, has been retired to a back field. This piece of equipment was used to rake hay into piles in preparation for baling.

MAPLE SUGARING >>

TOPSFIELD

PAUL WATSON
33 MM, KODAK E100 VS

Covered galvanized buckets collect the sap from sugar maple trees. Forty gallons of sap will boil down to just one gallon of pure maple syrup. There were 214 farms in Massachusetts that produced 44,000 gallons of syrup in 1999.

OTIS POULTRY FARM

OTIS

MARGARETA THAUTE
NIKON N90S, FUJI PROVIA

Cattle at the Otis Poultry Farm take a drink from a recycled bathtub. This farm has been a family business since 1904. They have a retail shop where you can purchase fresh eggs, pies, candy and other farm products.

WOOLY SITUATION

GREAT BARRINGTON

MARGARETA THAUTE
NIKON N90S, FUJI PROVIA

Four of the approximate nine thousand sheep in Massachusetts hang out in Great Barrington waiting to do their part for the wool industry.

TWIN SILOS >>

GREAT BARRINGTON

MARGARETA THAUTE
NIKON N90S, FUJI PROVIA

A traditional red barn with two silos to store food for livestock. Fodder, often finely chopped hay, is harvested while green and kept succulent by the fermentation process that occurs in silos.

SPRING BARN

GREAT BARRINGTON

MARGARETA THAUTE
NIKON N90S, FUJI PROVIA

This aging barn has seen better days. The lightning rods atop these buildings may have protected them from lightning strikes but the passage of time is obvious in the missing glass and boards.

STILL LIFE WORKBENCH »

WILBRAHAM

DOUGLAS R. AMENDE
MINOLTA 700SI, FUJI VELVIA F-22

The items discarded on shelves in this old barn are clues to its history.

CRANBERRY HARVEST

CARVER

DOUGLAS R. AMENDE
MINOLTA 700SI, FUJI VELVIA F-22

Cranberries and a pumpkin—the fruits of an autumn harvest.

BARN DOOR »

ERGERMONT

MARGARETA THAUTE
NIKON N90S, FUJI PROVIA

This peeling barn door hasn't been opened in quite a while.

photo by: Karen Crook Matt...

CONTRIBUTORS